Christina Litwiller

DIVINE PRESENCE AMID VIOLENCE

OTHER BOOKS BY WALTER BRUEGGEMANN

⌣

A Pathway of Interpretation

Praying the Psalms, 2nd edition

Ichabod toward Home: The Journey of God's Glory

In Man We Trust: The Neglected Side of Biblical Faith

To Act Justly, Love Tenderly, Walk Humbly:
An Agenda for Ministers

Theology of the Old Testament: Testimony, Dispute, Advocacy

Old Testament Theology: Essays on Structure, Theme, and Text

Like Fire in the Bones: Listening for the Prophetic Word in Jeremiah

The Word that Describes the World: The Bible and Discipleship

The Word Militant: Preaching a Decentering World

Awed to Heaven, Rooted to Earth: Prayers of Walter Brueggemann

The Book That Breathes New Life:
Scriptural Authority and Biblical Theology

Interpretation and Obedience:
From Faithful Reading to Faithful Living

Divine Presence amid Violence

Contextualizing the Book of Joshua

WALTER BRUEGGEMANN

CASCADE *Books* · Eugene, Oregon

DIVINE PRESENCE AMID VIOLENCE
Contextualizing the Book of Joshua

Cascade Books
A Division of Wipf and Stock Publishers
199 W. 8th Ave., Suite 3
Eugene, OR 97401

www.wipfandstock.com

ISBN 13: 978-1-60608-089-4

Cataloging-in-publication data:

Brueggemann, Walter.
Divine presence amid violence : contextualizing the book of Joshua /
Walter Brueggemann.

xii + 82 p. ; 20 cm. Includes bibliographical references and index.

Eugene, Ore.: Cascade Books

ISBN 13: 978-1-60608-089-4

1. War—Biblical teaching. 2. Bible. O.T. Joshua—Criticism,
interpretation, etc. 3. Revelation. I. Title.

BS1199 W2 B78 2009

Manufactured in the U.S.A.

For

Marilyn Stavenger

I am delighted to dedicate this book to Marilyn Stavenger,
my longtime comrade in ministry. Marilyn has modeled
critical generosity in ministry that is respectful, dialogical, and
empowering. It is appropriate that she be mentioned in this book
because her generous feminism has lived out a faithful life of
nonviolent transformative power. I am glad to count her a dear
friend and treasured companion in ministry.

Contents

Introduction

The conviction that Scripture is revelatory literature is a constant, abiding conviction among the communities of Jews and Christians that gather around the book.[1] But that conviction, constant and abiding as it is, is problematic and open to a variety of alternative and often contradictory or ambiguous meanings.[2] Clearly that conviction is appropriated differently in various contexts and various cultural settings.[3] Current attention to hermeneutics convinces many of us that there is no single, sure meaning for any text. The revelatory power of the text is discerned and given precisely through the action of interpretation which is always concrete, never universal, always contextualized, never "above the fray," always filtered through vested interest, never in disinterested purity.[4]

1. Tracy has usefully interpreted this conviction in terms of the Bible as a "classic"; *The Analogical Imagination*, chapters 3–7.

2. See Kelsey, *The Uses of Scripture in Recent Theology*.

3. Sobrino has shown how "the Enlightenment" as a context of interpretation can be handled in two very different ways, depending on whether one organizes the matter around Kant or Marx; *The True Church and the Poor*, 10–21. Obviously Kant and Marx were interested in very different notions of what may be enlightened, and the implications for interpretation lead in very different directions. This difference is illustrative of the interpretive options more generally available.

4. Habermas has shown how all knowledge is related to matters of

If that is true for the interpretive end of the process that receives the text, we may entertain the notion that it is also true for the interpretive end of the process that forms, shapes, and offers the text. That is, not only in its hearing, but also in its speaking, the text makes its disclosure in ways that are concrete, contextualized, and filtered through vested interest. While this leaves open the charge of relativism, it is in fact only a candid acknowledgment of the central conviction around which historical-critical studies have revolved for two hundred years. Historical-critical studies have insisted that a text can only be understood in context; historical-critical study believes historical context is necessary to hearing the text. But our objectivist ideology has uncritically insisted that knowledge of historical context of a text would allow us to be objective interpreters without recognizing that from its very inception, the textual process is not and cannot be objective.[5]

Historical-critical study thus gives us access to a certain interpretive act that generates the text, but that original interpretive act is not objective. This acknowledgment of the formation of the text as a constructive event is a recognition of what we know about ourselves, that we are not only meaning receivers, but we are also meaning makers. We not only accept meanings offered, but we construct meanings that we

---

interest, and that any imagined objectivity is likely to be an exercise in self-deception; *Knowledge and Human Interests*. On such presumed objectivity, see Schüssler Fiorenza, *Bread Not Stone*; idem, *Rhetoric and Ethic: The Politics of Biblical Studies*.

5. See the helpful statement by Dorr, *Spirituality and Justice*.

advocate.[6] The receiving, constructing act of interpretation changes both us and the text. This suggests that Scripture as revelation is never simply a final disclosure, but is an ongoing act of disclosing that will never let the disclosure be closed. The disclosing process is an open interaction with choices exercised in every step of interpretation from formation to reception.

Elsewhere I have summarized our situation with regard to knowing and interpretation:

> In place of objective certitude and settled hegemony, we would now characterize our knowing in ways that make mastery and control much more problematic, if indeed mastery and control can any longer be our intention at all. I would characterize our new intellectual situation in these rather obvious ways:
>
> 1. Our knowing is inherently *contextual*. This should hardly come to us as a surprise. Descartes wanted to insist that context was not relevant to knowing. It is, however, now clear that what one knows and sees depends upon where one stands or sits . . .
>
> 2. It follows that contexts are quite *local*, and the more one generalizes, the more one loses or fails to notice context. Localism means that it is impossible to voice large truth. All one can do is to voice local truth and propose that it pertains elsewhere. In fact, I should insist that all our

---

6. On the human person (and derivatively the human community) as a constructor of meanings, see Kegan, *The Evolving Self*; Schafer, *Language and Insight*; and Berger and Luckmann, *The Social Construction of Reality*.

knowing is quite local, even when we say it in a loud voice . . .

3. It follows from contextualism and localism that knowledge is inherently *pluralistic*, a cacophony of claims, each of which rings true to its own advocates. Indeed, pluralism is the only alternative to objectivism once the dominant center is no longer able to impose its view and to silence by force all alternative or dissenting opinion.[7]

---

7. Brueggemann, *Texts under Negotiation*, 8–9.

When King Jabin of Hazor heard of this, he sent to King Jobab of Madon, to the king of Shimron, to the king of Achshaph, 2 and to the kings who were in the northern hill country, and in the Arabah south of Chinneroth, and in the lowland, and in Naphoth-dor on the west, 3 to the Canaanites in the east and the west, the Amorites, the Hittites, the Perizzites, and the Jebusites in the hill country, and the Hivites under Hermon in the land of Mizpah. 4 They came out, with all their troops, a great army, in number like the sand on the seashore, with very many horses and chariots. 5 All these kings joined their forces, and came and camped together at the waters of Merom, to fight with Israel.

6 And the LORD said to Joshua, "Do not be afraid of them, for tomorrow at this time I will hand over all of them, slain, to Israel; you shall hamstring their horses, and burn their chariots with fire." 7 So Joshua came suddenly upon them with all his fighting force, by the waters of Merom, and fell upon them. 8 And the LORD handed them over to Israel, who attacked them and chased them as far as Great Sidon and Misrephoth-maim, and eastward as far as the valley of Mizpeh. They struck them down, until they had left no one remaining. 9 And Joshua did to them as the LORD commanded him; he hamstrung their horses, and burned their chariots with fire.

10 Joshua turned back at that time, and took Hazor, and struck its king down with the sword. Before that time Hazor was the head of all those kingdoms. 11 And they put to the sword all who were in it, utterly destroying them; there was no one left who breathed, and he

burned Hazor with fire. ¹² And all the towns of those kings, and all their kings, Joshua took, and struck them with the edge of the sword, utterly destroying them, as Moses the servant of the Lord had commanded. ¹³ But Israel burned none of the towns that stood on mounds except Hazor, which Joshua did burn. ¹⁴ All the spoil of these towns, and the livestock, the Israelites took for their booty; but all the people they struck down with the edge of the sword, until they had destroyed them, and they did not leave any who breathed. ¹⁵ As the Lord had commanded his servant Moses, so Moses commanded Joshua, and so Joshua did; he left nothing undone of all that the Lord had commanded Moses.

¹⁶ So Joshua took all that land: the hill country and all the Negeb and all the land of Goshen and the lowland and the Arabah and the hill country of Israel and its lowland, ¹⁷ from Mount Halak, which rises toward Seir, as far as Baal-gad in the valley of Lebanon below Mount Hermon. He took all their kings, struck them down, and put them to death. ¹⁸ Joshua made war a long time with all those kings. ¹⁹ There was not a town that made peace with the Israelites, except the Hivites, the inhabitants of Gibeon; all were taken in battle. ²⁰ For it was the Lord's doing to harden their hearts so that they would come against Israel in battle, in order that they might be utterly destroyed, and might receive no mercy, but be exterminated, just as the Lord had commanded Moses.

²¹ At that time Joshua came and wiped out the Anakim from the hill country, from Hebron, from Debit, from Anab, and from all the hill country of Judah, and from all the hill country of Israel; Joshua utterly destroyed them with their towns. ²² None of the Anakim was left in the land of the Israelites; some remained only in Gaza, in Gath, and in Ashdod. ²³ So Joshua took the whole land, according to all that the Lord had spoken to Moses; and Johua gave it for an inheritance to Israel according to their tribabl allotments. And the land had rest from war.

1 *Revelation, Interpretation, and Method*

Two methods of Scripture interpretation that emerged in the late twentieth century are important for the relation between revelation and interpretation. I want to consider both of these methods in relation to the revelatory character of the text.

The first of these methods is sociology—or more broadly, social-scientific criticism: this includes especially macrosociology and cultural anthropology.[1] It has become apparent that much historical-critical study has focused on the question of facticity to so large an extent that it has bracketed out questions of social process, social interest, and social possibility. A number of studies have made use of tools of social analysis to ask about the social intention and social function of a text in relation to the community and the situation upon which the text impinges.[2] Among the more important of these studies are:

---

1. See the summary statement of Wilson, *Sociological Approaches to the Old Testament*; Overholt, *Cultural Anthropology and the Old Testament*; and Carter, "Social Scientific Approaches."

2. A helpful example of how sociological analysis may shape exegetical interpretation is offered in *God of the Lowly*, edited by Schottroff and Stegemann.

- Norman K. Gottwald on the early period,[3]

- James W. Flanagan on David,[4]

- Robert R. Wilson and Thomas W. Overholt on the prophets,[5]

- Paul D. Hanson on the later exilic and post-exilic periods,[6]

- Jon L. Berquist on the Persian era,[7]

- Carol Meyers on women in ancient Israel,[8]

- Lester L. Grabbe on "religious specialists."[9]

A programmatic formula for such an enterprise is that it is a "materialist" reading,[10] a phrase Gottwald would accept for his work, but perhaps some of the others mentioned would not. A "materialist reading" suggests that the text cannot be separated from the social processes out of which it emerged. The text also is a product of the community. The community that generates the text is engaged in production of the text, and the community that reads it is engaged in consumption

---

3. Gottwald, *The Tribes of Yahweh*; see also his *The Hebrew Bible: A Socio-literary Introduction*.

4. Flanagan, *David's Social Drama*.

5. Wilson, *Prophecy and Society in Ancient Israel*; Overholt, *Channels of Prophecy*.

6. Hanson, *The Dawn of Apocalyptic*.

7. Berquist, *Judaism in Persia's Shadow*.

8. Meyers, *Discovering Eve*; and *Households and Holiness*.

9. Grabbe, *Priests, Prophets, Diviners, Sages*.

10. See Füssel, "The Materialist Reading of the Bible"; and more generally, Clevenot, *Materialist Approaches to the Bible*.

of the text, so that the text needs to be discussed according to processes of production and consumption.[11] In what follows, I will want to consider a materialist reading of a text, as an attempt to appropriate its revelatory claim. The text as product for consumption suggests the operation of intentionality and interest in the shaping of the text.

The second emerging method that will be useful for us is literary analysis. Literary analysis seeks to take the text on its own terms as an offer of meaning, as an exercise in creative imagination to construct a world that does not exist apart from the literary act of the text.[12] The nuances of the text are not simply imaginative literary moves, but are acts of world-making that create and evoke an alternative world available only through this text. The authoritative voices in such a method are

- Paul Ricoeur, from the perspective of hermeneutics[13]

- Amos Wilder, from the perspective of rhetoric.[14]

In Old Testament studies, among the more effective efforts at analyses of literature as "making worlds" are those of:

11. Leonardo Boff has applied these categories to the sacramental life of the church, even as Füssel has applied them to the character of the text; see Boff, *Church: Charisma and Power*, 110–15.

12. For a critical assessment of this interpretive view as it pertains to biblical interpretation, see Barton, *Reading the Old Testament*.

13. Ricoeur's work is scattered in many places, but see especially *Interpretation Theory*; *The Conflict of Interpretations*; and *The Philosophy of Paul Ricoeur*. See also Crossan, editor, *Paul Ricoeur on Biblical Hermeneutics*.

14. For a most helpful introduction to Wilder's view of literature as world-making, see Wilder, "Story and Story-World."

- David Gunn[15]

- David J. A. Clines[16]

- Phyllis Trible[17]

- Robert Alter[18]

- Meir Sternberg.[19]

This literary approach seeks to receive the world offered in the text, even if that world is distant from and incongruent with our own. Thus the text is not a report on a world "out there," but is an offer of another world that is evoked in and precisely by the text. The text "reveals" a world that would not be disclosed apart from this text. This view suggests that the alternative to the world of this text is not an objective world out there, but it is another "evoked world" from another text,[20] albeit a text that may be invisible and unrecognized by us. We are always choosing between texts, and the interpretive act is to see the ways in which the world disclosed in this text is a compelling "sense-making" world.[21] Literary analysis

---

15. Gunn, *The Fate of King Saul*; and *The Story of King David*.

16. See especially Clines, *I, He, We and They*.

17. Trible, *God and the Rhetoric of Sexuality*, *Texts of Terror*, and *Rhetorical Criticism*.

18. Alter, *The Art of Biblical Narrative*.

19. Sternberg, *The Poetics of Biblical Narrative*.

20. Myers has shown how the work of Hobbes is "the text" for Adam Smith, which in turn has become the text for the capitalist world, even if unacknowledged; *The Soul of Modern Economic Man*.

21. On the active power of "sense-making" as the production of sense, see Jobling, *The Sense of Biblical Narrative*, especially 1–3; and Brueggemann, "As the Text 'Makes Sense,'" 7–10.

assumes that the text is not a one-dimensional statement, but is an offer of a world that has an interiority, in which the text is not a monolithic voice, but is a conversation out of which comes a new world.

When one puts the social-scientific and literary methods together in a common interpretive act,[22] it is clear that the voices in the text may speak and be heard and interpreted in various ways. Some voices may be shrill, arid, domineering; some may be willingly quiet; some may be silenced and defeated. It is, nonetheless, the entire conversation in the text that discloses an alternative world for us. Thus Scripture as revelation is not a flat, obvious offer of a conclusion, but it is an ongoing conversation that evokes, invites, and offers. It is the process of the text itself, in which each interpretive generation participates, that is the truth of revelation. Such an interaction is not a contextless activity but the context is kept open and freshly available, depending on the social commitments of the interpreter and the sense-making conversations heard in the act of interpretation. In this strange interpretive process, we dare to claim and confess that God's fresh word and new truth are mediated and made available to us.

It will be clear from the foregoing that my assumption is that there are no "innocent" readings of Scripture, and surely there are no "innocent" formations of Scripture. This is not to reduce the witness or interpretation of Scripture to vested interest, but it is to insist that every faithful witness and interpretation is to some extent filtered through and impinged

22. See my attempt at such a methodological interface in Brueggemann, *David's Truth*; *Theology of the Old Testament*; and most recently in *A Pathway of Interpretation*.

upon by the interpreter. One way of recognizing that "truth" is impacted by "power" is to see that every text is a carrier of interest that voices truth from a certain perspective. Of course the generic name for that reality is "ideology," even though the term itself is more than a little problematic. On the one hand "ideology" is a gift from Karl Marx, who proposed that articulations of truth from above are characteristically done in bad faith, because they reflect particular interests, and characteristically seek to disguise that interest in language that deceives. Freud, of course, went further with his perception of the ways in which human persons have the power to self-deceive. On the other hand, a much more benign notion of ideology is fostered by the anthropologist Clifford Geertz, who understands the term to refer to any sense-making account of reality, so that it need not necessarily be an articulation of bad faith or deceit.[23] In that usage the term "ideology" serves as a synonym for elemental social conviction, or even theological conviction, a passionate articulation of an overall meaning. Of course the distinction between the two uses is slippery, and there is a tendency to judge that even a "benign ideology" may serve a special pleading.

In any use, any awareness of ideology at all serves to alert one that texts are not to be read and trusted with straightforward claims, but that one must ask what the text and the interpretation of the text seek to do in the act of interpretation. It is for that reason that critical studies of late have become much interested in ideology critique as a counter to the kind of historical criticism that has tended toward positivism. The

23. Geertz, "Ideology as a Cultural System."

methods I have identified—rhetorical criticism and social-scientific criticism—recognize that every interpretation—and every text—is an act designed to accomplish something. Ideology critique is an effort to exercise a kind of hermeneutic of suspicion that does not dismiss the text in a skeptical way, but that recognizes that texts not only *say,* but *do.*

Once one has recognized that texts *do* as well as *say,* it is useful to refer to the rubric of my *Theology of the Old Testament* with its subthesis of "testimony, dispute, and advocacy." I have utilized these terms in order to explicate Old Testament theology because I have come to view the Old Testament (and its interpretive trajectories) as a contestation about the truth of God and of God's world. The juridical terms I have employed suggest that the text and its interpretations are an ongoing act to determine what is true. There I have suggested

- that *testimony* is a verbal account of reality that bears witness to a certain version of reality;

- that such testimony is inescapably in *dispute* with other versions of reality that are also attested,

- so that every version of reality—each text and each interpretation—vis-à-vis other texts and other interpretations *advocates* a certain version of reality that seeks to challenge and refute other versions.

It is for that reason that I have utilized a juridical metaphor for Old Testament theology, because texts are like witnesses that trace out the character of Yahweh against other characterizations of Yahweh, and thereby advocate a certain rendering of reality.

The upshot of this view of method, ideology, and testimony–dispute–advocacy is the recognition that every text makes its claim. Each such claim, moreover, requires attention, that it be recognized and understood and weighed alongside other texts with other claims. Such a perspective on biblical texts sees the "canon" as a venue for contestation. It takes the canon seriously but recognizes that the canonical literature does not offer a settled, coherent account of reality; rather it provides the materials for ongoing disputatious interpretation. Any consideration of the "culture wars" of our society—wherein both sides appeal to biblical texts—makes clear that the biblical text is a venue for contestation and that the texts themselves are grist for the dispute. In what follows I consider a text that surely is to be understood as thick with ideology, but that nonetheless is a carrier of "a disclosure" of the Holy One of Israel.

2 *Discerning Revelation from God*

To pursue this matter of "revelation in context," I will address an exceedingly difficult text in the Old Testament, Joshua 11. The reason for taking up this text is to deal with the often asked and troublesome question: What shall we do with all the violence and bloody war that is done in the Old Testament in the name of Yahweh?[1] The question reflects a sense that these texts of violence are at least an embarrassment, are morally repulsive, and are theologically problematic in the Bible, not because they are violent, but because this is violence either in the name of or at the hand of Yahweh.

The questions we shall consider are the following: How are these texts of violence to be understood as revelation? What is it that is disclosed? And how shall this disclosure be received as serious, authoritative, and binding as the only rule for life and faith? We shall consider the revelatory question in two dimensions. The first is revelation within the text. What

1. On the general question, see P. D. Miller, "God the Warrior"; P. D. Hanson, "War and Peace in the Hebrew Bible"; Bergant, "Peace in a Universe of Order"; and von Waldow, "The Concept of War in the Old Testament." The journals in which the Hanson and von Waldow articles appear have entire issues devoted to the subject of war and peace in the Bible. See also Good, "The Just War in Ancient Israel"; von Rad, *Holy War in Ancient Israel*; Craigie, *The Problem of War in the Old Testament*; Jones, "The Concept of Holy War"; and Collins, *Does the Bible Justify Violence?*

has drawn me to Joshua 11 is the awareness that within the text as such very little, surprisingly little, is directly assigned to Yahweh as revelation. So we ask how the characters in this text discerned God's revelation. Second, we shall go on to ask about how the whole of the text is taken as revelation, once the text is stabilized for us. It may well be that this distinction will be useful in understanding how this text should be handled in faith communities that celebrate revelation but flinch from violence linked to God. The warrant for violence within the text may yield a very different disclosure when we take the text as a stable revelatory unit. In our text, what Joshua and ancient Israel took as revelation may provide a clue for our hearing the text as revelatory. But the two may not be identified or equated.

It is clear that this text, like every biblical text, has no fixed, closed meaning; it is inescapably open to interpretation that reflects specific circumstance and location. In this case, the Joshua material in the thirteenth century (if the text were that old) may have "revealed" a divine intent about "conquest." But in the fifth century, the likely time of the final form of the text, the revelatory dimension would have been read with much less attention to the raw assertion of divine agency through violence against the Canaanites. In our own time, moreover, these texts may assert divine resolve and intentionality, but very many readers cringe from the divine readiness for violence. Thus, whatever is taken as revelatory in this text in our circumstance, it is certain that the articulation of divine violence is an acute awkwardness. Very often interpretation labors to "explain away" such a characterization of God, not least because contemporary interpreters are increasingly aware of the abusive character of much religion in the name of God. The revelatory claim for the text may be that this God wills for God's chosen that they should not be landless in the world. But that claim in contemporary context is fraught with immense problems. As Regina Schwartz has argued, the very notion of "chosenness" carries with it implications of violence that remain definingly problematic.[2] For that reason our contemporary interpretation of such texts must be knowing about our own time and place. The text cannot be taken as an absolute outside of time, but is always drawn into particular time and place by the act of interpretation.

We may begin with a summary of some standard critical observations.[3] The first half of the book of Joshua (chapters 1–12) concerns the conquest of the land, which is ordered by God. Chapters 13–22 concern the division of the land, ordered by Joshua. The book of Joshua is a theological account in which God acts directly as an agent in the narrative. Within Joshua 1–12, the specific narrative accounts concern

- 2 and 6: *the conquest of Jericho*

- 3 and 4: *the crossing at Gilgal*

- 5: *the institution of circumcision*

- 7 and 8:1–29: *the crisis of Achan and Ai*

2. Schwartz, *The Curse of Cain*.

3. For a summary of the critical discussion, see Childs, *Introduction to the Old Testament as Scripture*, 239–44; and Collins, *An Introduction to the Hebrew Bible*, 183–202. For detailed commentaries, see Boling and Wright, *Joshua*; Butler, *Joshua*; Coote, "The Book of Joshua"; Gray, *Joshua, Judges, and Ruth*; and Nelson, *Joshua*.

- 8:30–35: *the altar on Mt. Ebal near Shechem*

- 9: *the subservience of the Gibeonites*

- 10: *the taking of the south.*

Albrecht Alt has suggested that these narratives conclude with etiological formulas that evidence that they were originally teaching tales to justify present phenomena. He has observed that these etiological narratives tend to be located in a narrow geographical range with particular reference to the tribal area of Benjamin.[4]

Joshua 1; 11:16–23; and 12 are more general statements that make more sweeping claims. It seems apparent that chapters 1 and 12 are placed as a theological envelope for the more specific accounts. Chapter 11 tends to move toward a comprehensive summary (vv. 16–23), but focuses on the specific matter of Hazor, the great city of the north (vv. 1–15).[5] Thus it has affinities with the generalizations of chapter 12, but also balances the southern account of chapter 10 with this northern report on Hazor.[6] To the extent that this chapter generalizes, it may also reflect Deuteronomistic stylization.

Within chapter 11 we may present an overview of the following elements:

4. Cf. Alt, "Joshua."

5. We will consider both parts of the chapter in order to attend to the dynamics of the text. In critical analysis, the first part of the chapter is a specific narrative, whereas the latter part is a general theological summary. Literarily the two parts serve very different functions.

6. See Boling and Wright, *Joshua*, 303–14, for the notion of a two-stage presentation of the conquest. See the general discussion of Noth, *The Deuteronomistic History*, 36–41.

1. In vv. 1–5 the king of Hazor takes the initiative in mobilizing many other kings to resist Israel. It is important that in this case it is not Israel who is the aggressor.[7] The inventory of mobilized kings must be a generalized and stylized list. It includes kings of the north, kings of the south, and kingdoms that characteristically occur in the stereotypical Deuteronomistic list of seven kingdoms (Deut 7:1; 20:17). Thus the list is not to be taken as historically literal. And it seems to be written as a parallel to the coalition, described in Joshua 10:1–5, that was mustered by king Adoni-zedek of Jerusalem. What interests us about the list is that it reflects the power of city-states, armed with "many horses and chariots."

Following the general analysis of Gottwald,[8] the city-states are to be understood as monopolies of socioeconomic, political power that are managed in hierarchal and oppressive ways. Many of these were remnants of the city-states set-up and controlled by Egypt. We have a window on these arrangements in the more than three hundred letters discovered in Tel el-Amarna (the collection is abbreviated EA) coming from the fourteenth century BCE.[9] "Horses and chariots" reflect the strength and monopoly of arms that are necessary and available for the maintenance of the economic and political monopoly.[10] Note the Amarna letter from the king of

7. See Boling and Wright, *Joshua*, 303.

8. Gottwald, *The Tribes of Yahweh*, 389–419. See also Mendenhall, "The Hebrew Conquest of Palestine."

9. For translations, see Moran, *The Amarna Letters*.

10. See Gottwald, *The Tribes of Yahweh*, 542–43. Boling and Wright, *Joshua*, 307, suggest only that chariots are "new-fangled" and therefore Israel did not have them. I suggest that such a chronological explanation

Alashiya (Cyprus) to the Egyptian Pharaoh, which demonstrates how horses and chariots were symbols of royal power and prosperity: "And may it be well with my brother. With your houses, your wives, your sons, your chief men, your horses, your chariots, and in your lands, may it be well" (EA 35:5–8).

2. Verses 16–20 composes a summary that roughly corresponds to the summary of vv. 1–5: "So Joshua took all that land . . ."[11] There (vv. 1–5) we have the list of enemies of Israel. Here (vv. 16–20) we are told that Joshua defeated all of them; note the parallel to the concluding summary in 10:40–43.

3. Verses 21–23 provide an expanded observation concerning the Anakim who were defeated, except in cities assigned to Philistia: "At that time Joshua came and wiped out the Anakim . . ." (v. 21). This section, according to Noth, is Deuteronomistic. It makes a transition to the distribution of land in what follows, and it ends with the standard formula about rest in the land: "And the land had rest from war" (v. 23). Thus in vv. 1–5 and 16–23 we have sweeping generalizations that frame the chapter that is built around an older story. There has been a great effort against Israel who, with

misses the point of the theological and social practice to which Israel is committed.

11. Boling and Wright, *Joshua*, 316, consider this as belonging to the Deuteronomist; Noth, *The Deuteronomistic History*, 38, refers to a "compiler" and assigns v. 20b to the Deuteronomist. For our purposes, such a refinement of literary analysis is neither necessary nor useful.

the intervention of Yahweh, has won despite enormous odds against them.

4. In vv. 6–9 we have the central narrative element of the text:

The command of Yahweh: "And Yahweh said to Joshua, 'Do not be afraid of them, for tomorrow at this time I will hand over all of them, slain, to Israel; you shall hamstring their horses, and burn their chariots with fire'" (v. 6).

The responsive action of Joshua: "So Joshua came suddenly upon them with all his fighting force, by the waters of Merom, and fell upon them. And Yahweh handed them over to Israel, who attacked them and chased them as far as Great Sidon and Misrephoth-maim, and eastward as far as the valley of Mizpeh. They struck them down, until they had left no one remaining" (vv. 7–8).

And the concluding formula that Joshua obeyed the command of Yahweh: "And Joshua did to them as Yahweh commanded him; he hamstrung their horses, and burned their chariots with fire" (v. 9).

This unit is of particular interest because v. 6 is the only speech of Yahweh in the entire chapter—indeed the only speech from anyone. All the rest is narrative. For our interest in revelation, we may expect that this speech element will be of particular importance.

5. In vv. 10–15 we have a battle report concerning the actual conquest of Hazor, whose king had made the initial move toward war in v. 1: "Joshua turned back at that time, and took Hazor, and struck its king down with the sword" (v. 10). These verses are of special interest, as Polzin has seen, because of the settlement made on the traditional command of *ḥerem*.[12]

Thus chapter 11 is framed by a general summary (vv. 1–5, 16–23). The latter part of the envelope may not all be of a piece, but it is all summary. Inside the framework are two, much more specific, statements that concern us: vv. 6–9 on command and obedience, and vv. 10–15 on the destruction of Hazor and the problem of *ḥerem*. Even though the chapter tends to be handled as a generalizing conclusion, there is little here that is specifically Deuteronomistic. The parts that concern us stand largely free of that influence, except perhaps the formula of obedience in v. 10.

---

12. Polzin, *Moses and the Deuteronomist*, 123–26. On *ḥerem*, see Stern, *The Biblical Ḥerem*; Kang, *Divine War*; and Niditch, *War in the Hebrew Bible*.

3 *Divine Permit*

I understand monarchy in Israel, or among its neighbors, to be a political concentration of power and an economic monopoly of wealth.[1] When monarchy appears in Israel, it comes along with such concentration and monopoly, though of course there are important models available for royal Israel prior to David and Solomon. Such concentrations and monopolies have to be maintained and therefore defended, because such monopoly is not welcomed by everyone, especially those who are disadvantaged by it and exploited for it.

Interestingly, Norman K. Gottwald has suggested that the formation of the monarchy in Israel (so disputed in 1 Samuel 7–15) is not simply defense against the Philistines, as is a conventional view among scholars, but is the necessary and predictable political counterpart of a growing economic surplus and monopoly.[2] That is, the state did not gather the surplus, but the accumulated, disproportionate surplus necessitated the state in order to legitimate, maintain, and protect a surplus that was already partly in hand. And it should be noted that "surplus" does not refer to "wealth" but is a social-

1. For a model of aristocratic empires, see K. C. Hanson and Oakman, *Palestine in the Time of Jesus*, 64. See also Chaney, "Systematic Study of the Israelite Monarchy."

2. Gottwald, "Social History of the United Monarchy."

scientific term meaning anything beyond what is necessary for subsistence.

In Joshua 11, of course, we have no Israelite monarchy. But we do have monarchies, which in this narrative are antagonistic to Israel. Following the model of Gottwald, I regard "Israel" as an antimonarchic, peasant movement hostile to every concentration, surplus, and monopoly. Conversely it follows then that every such city-state as those listed in vv. 1–5 would regard Israel as a threat, for Israel practiced a social alternative that had to be destroyed. Thus we can read the mobilization of the Hazor king with sociological realism as a conflict between competing social systems.[3] The initiative of the king of Hazor is preemptive, perhaps not unlike the Bush administration's initiative against the alleged growing threat of the "weapons of mass destruction" in Iraq.

We may begin our textual analysis by noting the three-fold reference to "horses and chariots" in this narrative. First, in v. 4, the military mobilization of city-states is routinely described as "horses and chariots." Israel has none, for horses and chariots are tools of states and empires, necessary and paid for in order to guard the monopoly. That is a given in this ancient society. Note that in a subsequent text Solomon is described as being a monarch who not only marshaled a large contingent of horses and chariots for himself, but also became

---

3. Boling and Wright, *Joshua*, 310, come close to such a conclusion when they speaks of "the royal families and ruling aristocracies," and then of the "peasants." They have not, in my judgment, pursued far enough the implications of such a social analysis.

a broker of them to other kingdoms (1 Kgs 10:26–29).[4] As Kautsky observes:

> Initially, warfare may be carried on to expand the holdings and thus the income of the aristocracy, but then it continues also to protect the area controlled by the aristocracy from warlike tribes and rival aristocracies. With each ruling aristocracy necessarily suspicious of the others, because each can maintain itself only by being ready for war and thus by threatening the others, preventive wars and wars of prestige are added to wars carried on for expansion and for defense.[5]

In v. 6, "horses and chariots" are mentioned a second time, this time in a statement by Yahweh:

> Do not be afraid of them, for tomorrow at this time I will hand over all of them, slain, to Israel. You shall hamstring the horses and burn the chariots with fire.

This is a remarkably interesting speech.[6] First it is an assurance: "do not fear." It is as though Yahweh recognizes how dangerous the situation is for Israel, because the military contest is a hopeless mismatch. It is an uneven match because the city-states have advanced military technology, and Israel

---

4. See Brueggemann, *Solomon.*

5. Kautsky, *The Politics of Aristocratic Empires,* 145.

6. Conrad, "The 'Fear Not' Oracles in Second Isaiah," has greatly contributed to our understanding of this genre of speech. See more extensively Conrad, *Fear Not Warrior.* Conrad has shown how the formula may yield either an assurance or a command. In our text, it yields both. Cf. Conrad, *Fear Not Warrior,* 8–10.

has no access to such technology. The only counter to military technology, according to the narrative, is the powerful liberating voice of Yahweh. Second, as often following "do not fear," there is a promise of a quite specific kind, introduced by, "for tomorrow I am handing them over all of them, slain, to Israel."[7] Third, after the promise and the assurance is the command, with the word order inverted, forming a chiasmus with the promise for accent:

> Their horses you will hamstring, their chariots you
> will burn in fire.

This speech (v. 6) is at the center of our interest in revelation, for it is God's only speech in this chapter. This speech, including assurance, promise, and command, is addressed only to Joshua the leader, not the troops as in Deuteronomy 20:2–4. All the real action in this unit is to be done by Israelites, who are to sabotage and immobilize the imperial weapons of war. Yahweh undertakes no direct action. We should note that in this direct command, the only object of violence is horses and chariots, i.e., weapons. There is nothing here about burning cities, killing kings or people, or seizing war booty. Yahweh's is a very lean mandate that addresses the simple, most important issue, the military threat of monarchal power against this alternative community lacking in military technology.

What we may most wonder about is what it is exactly that Yahweh promises to do. After the assurance and the rather nonspecific participle ("I am handing over"), Yahweh

---

7. On the function and power of the particle *kî* (in this passage translated "for"), see Muilenburg, "The Linguistic and Rhetorical Usages of the Particle *kî* in the Old Testament."

does nothing, but mandates Israel to do the action. I submit that a close reading shows Yahweh really does nothing in this verse and indeed does not promise to do anything beyond a general commitment of solidarity and legitimation. The action is left to Joshua and to Israel.

The third reference to "horses and chariots" (v. 9) reports that Joshua did as commanded and destroyed the military weapons of the military city-states. Thus there are three references to horses and chariots:

- The city kings had them (v. 4);

- Yahweh mandates their destruction (v. 6);

- Joshua destroys them as commanded (v. 9)

The first and third references are factual and descriptive, before and after the war. The second, in the mouth of Yahweh, is wondrously unlike the other two mentions. It is the speech of Yahweh. Here the text is not historically descriptive but theologically evocative. The disclosure is that Yahweh gave permission for Joshua and Israel to act for their justice and liberation against an oppressive adversary. This revelatory word of Yahweh, given directly without conduit or process, is only authorization for a liberating movement—which is sure to be violent, but only violent against weapons.

We do not know by what means this word has been given and received, and the narrative has no interest in that. We have examples in the Old Testament of such divine messages coming through an auditory address (Exod 3:4–6), a vision (Dan 5:5–31), a combination of an auditory address and vision (Amos 8:1–3), a dream (1 Kgs 3:5–15), or the casting of lots in response to a question (1 Sam 14:41–42). The best guess is that in this case it was an oracle to an officer, but that is to speculate outside the narrative presentation. But we do know that the disclosure of permit was taken seriously, not doubted, regarded as valid, and acted upon. What is revealed is that Yahweh is allied with the marginalized, oppressed peasants against the monopoly of the city-state. It is not a summons to violence (though its practice might be construed so) but only a permit that Joshua's community is entitled to dream, hope, and imagine freedom and is entitled to act upon that dream, hope, and imagination.[8] The Israelites, on any sociological analysis, were disadvantaged and oppressed. The permit of Yahweh authorized this community to act by hamstringing and burning for the sake of their own social destiny. Without such "permission" they would have continued in their oppressed, marginalized condition. Such revelatory permission is a counterpart to the "revolutionary impetus" of these narratives.

Now our focal question is to ask: Would the God of the Bible make such a disclosure as a permit for liberation that

8. On the psychology of granting and receiving permission, see Berne, *What Do You Say After You Say Hello?* 123–25; and *Beyond Games and Scripts*, 399, for a definition of the term in the context of one theory of therapy. "The granting of permission" can be done by one in authority to authorize another to act in freedom and courage against old patterns of coercion and repression. My colleague John Quigley has helped find these references and has also helped me see the dangerous distortion of the notion in popular usage with reference to ideological autonomy, which gives "permission" to do what one wants. But free of this distortion, I suggest, the notion illuminates our passage and the revelatory speech of Yahweh.

entailed violence against oppressive weapons and, by inference, against the systems that sanction such weapons?

1. We are bound to say that such a revelatory word is congruent with the fabric of Exodus faith, for Yahweh is there presented as a force for justice and liberation against concentrations of oppressive power. Yahweh's commitment is summarized in the slogan, "Let my people go" (Exod 5:1; 7:16; 8:1, 20; 9:1, 13; 10:3).

2. The disclosure of Yahweh is not intervention, but authorization. The claim of the narrative here is exceedingly modest. How indeed is liberation to happen in such a context? Israel, according to this narrative, is not recipient of a supernatural intervention. If justice and freedom are to come, Yahweh's way is through actual historical agents who act on their own behalf. That is what the text narrates. This rather obvious fact is of exceeding importance for the general interpretive posture taken here.

3. The authorization is the authorization of Joshua, his leadership, and his strategy. No one else has access to the disclosure. No one else heard the disclosure. No one else knows what was said. Revelation is linked to authorized communal authority, or in other categories, the revelation is the property of the agents that hold a monopoly of interpretation.[9]

9. On the monopoly of interpretation, the power and the problems it yields, see Kermode, *The Art of Telling*.

4. The disclosure from God that authorizes coheres with the dreams and yearning of this oppressed community, has credibility only in that community, and cannot be removed from that community for a more general statement. It was Israel's longstanding and courageous dream of an alternative social organization rooted in the memory of Moses that is the material and mode out of which revelation is articulated. Once this community has glimpsed the imaginative possibility of justice that it had glimpsed in the exodus, it could not understand itself unauthorized by God's disclosure. The disclosure that authorizes lives very close to the actual experience of the community. That is, revelation is not an act extrinsic to the social process, but it is an act precisely embedded in the social community.[10]

Instead of suggesting that revelation comes down to intrude in the community, I submit that this revelation arises up out of the hurt and the hope of this community, so that the dream is understood as certified from heaven, and as that dream is certified from heaven, it has enormous credibility in the life of the community on earth. The dream of liberation and justice has credibility theologically because to deny it is to deny everything Israel knows about Yahweh, the Lord of the Exodus. The revelatory word has credibility socially because the certitude of disclosure is not simply religious certitude, but a much more embedded, visceral, existential certitude

10. On the doing of theology that is embedded in local community experience, see Schreiter, *Constructing Local Theologies*.

that would not be denied. Israel knows deep in its own hurt and hope that this permit is God's truth and God's will.

Revelation for this community in the text is the convergence of:

- the old memory of liberation from the Exodus,[11]

- the peasant yearning for liberation and justice, and

- the formal speech reported by established leadership.

All three elements are indispensable. The disclosure cannot be denied because passion for liberating justice cannot be denied Yahweh, who is known in the Exodus tradition. The disclosure cannot be denied because the future social possibility is now unleashed in peasant imagination and will not be nullified. The disclosure cannot be denied because the authorization is reported on the lips of the authorized leader, Joshua, who is understood as fulfilling the function of Moses. The outcome is that no monarchic "horses and chariots" are permitted to stand in the way of such a promise from heaven or such a possibility on earth. All three elements—memory, yearning, and leadership—converge in this permit of Yahweh. Methodologically it is the peasant yearning that is the new and decisive ingredient in our understanding. It is this yearning publicly expressed that evokes the old memory in its

---

11. There is of course a methodological problem with making old memory a part of revelation, because it leaves open the charge of infinite regress. When one finally reaches the event behind which there is no old memory, that event is no doubt a theophany. On the reality of older memory in the faith of Israel, see the proposal of Gottwald, *The Tribes of Yahweh*, 483–97 and passim.

powerful authority and mobilizes the present leadership also accepted as authoritative.

The revelatory speech of Yahweh ends this way: "Hamstring the horses, burn the chariots with fire." When God speaks, we may expect something more respectable, something about "This is my beloved Son," or "Three persons and one substance," or "Grace alone, Scripture alone, Christ alone." But here it is "hamstring the horses."

In a classic essay, H. Richard Niebuhr has seen that revelation is embedded in community.[12] John L. McKenzie has argued more specifically the same way.[13] Both Niebuhr and McKenzie have seen that revelation and inspiration arise as a certitude given and received in a community. But it is characteristic of that generation of scholarship represented by Niebuhr and McKenzie that the notion of communities of revelation is understood without adequate reference to specific sociological circumstance.[14] That is, if communities mediate revelation from God, surely different communities in different circumstances will mediate different disclosures.

12. Niebuhr, *The Meaning of Revelation.*

13. McKenzie, "The Social Character of Inspiration."

14. The general notion of Niebuhr and McKenzie is inadequate because they did not reckon with the particularity of the community and therefore the particularity of its revelation. Each community operates through a particular rationality. If one ignores the socioeconomic particularity of a community, communities of marginality are likely to be thought of as irrational, so that their claim to have revelation is discredited. This dismissal of marginality as a habitat for revelation operates both sociologically and psychologically. On the latter, see Grant, *Schizophrenia*, who considers that the insights of schizophrenics may be revelational, even if an odd rationality that people with "horses and chariots" are likely to misunderstand and dismiss.

The community of the king of Hazor must have mediated God's intent for greater armed security. But to the community of Israel (understood as a community of marginality), which has given us this text we claim as revelatory, what God discloses is a permit or authorization to demobilize such royal arms that are threats to human welfare and specifically to the welfare of this community of marginality. If revelation is mediated through community, revelation will reflect the truth available to that community in its life, memory, and experience, and will tend therefore to be partisan disclosure. I submit that this community of oppressed peasants through which the winds of liberation blow could not mediate any other revelation from God and could not doubt this disclosure. The high God of eternity dwells with the lowly (Isa 57:15–16). For that reason, the God of these tribes decrees hamstringing horses as one concrete practice of truth. The truth of the disclosure is that it makes life possible for the community.

Except for Yahweh's permit and mandate in v. 6, all action in the narrative is left to Joshua and Israel. In their obedience to and trust in Yahweh's permit, Joshua and Israel do everything that is needful, while Yahweh does nothing. It is clear that Yahweh in fact does not "act" in this narrative, except in the important sense that the entire event occurs as Yahweh's act.[15] Yahweh made a promise in v. 6: "I will give over." In v. 8 that promise is kept: "And Yahweh gave them into the hand of Israel." We are not told what Yahweh did or how it was done.

15. On the problematic of "act of God," see Kaufman, "On the Meaning of 'Act of God'"; and Gilkey, "Cosmology, Ontology, and the Travail of Biblical Language."

Evidently Yahweh has authorized and legitimated, and that was enough. Even in v. 20, where the rhetoric is escalated, Yahweh does not act in a concrete way.

Thus I suggest that revelation in this narrative is not self-disclosure of God, for nothing new is shown of God; but revelation is the gift of authorization by which Joshua and Israel are legitimated for their own acts of liberation, which from the side of the king of Hazor are perceived as acts of violence. What is "disclosed" is that the world of the city-kings is not closed. It is the purpose of "horses and chariots" to close that world and so to render the peasants hopeless and helpless.[16] But the world ostensibly controlled by oppressive city-kings is now dis-closed, shown to be false, and broken open to the joy of Israel. The revelatory decree of Yahweh breaks the fixed world of city-kings. What we label as violence on Yahweh's part is a theological permit that sanctions a new social possibility.

That single, simple act of authorization is, religiously speaking, everything. It permits Israel to act. The main verbs of this chapter, therefore, have Israel, not Yahweh, as subject:

- They fell upon them (v. 7).

- They smote (vv. 8, 10, 14, 17).

- They utterly destroyed (vv. 11, 12, 20, 21).

16. See my chapter, "Blessed are the History-Makers," in *Hope within History*, 49–71. I have argued that "history-making" depends on vulnerability. Those who move from coercive strength are characteristically "history-stoppers" because they want to stop the ongoing conversation about power.

The word of Yahweh, given only to Joshua, created new historical, social possibilities for Israel, out of which Israel was able to act. The result is the complete transformation of the power situation of the world of Israel, a transformation wrought by the direct active intervention of Israel, not of Yahweh.

This is not to make a liberal claim that "God has no hands but ours"—Yahweh does the one thing needful. Yahweh legitimates self-assertion on the part of the powerless. The juxtaposition of God's power and human power needs to be nuanced very differently among those with horses and chariots. But this is not their text.

Commenting on the traditions of Yahweh's liberation of Israel in the exodus traditions I have said,

> This most radical of all of Israel's testimony about Yahweh verifies that the God of Israel is a relentless opponent of human oppression, even when oppression is untaken and sponsored by what appear to be legitimated powers. Thus Yahweh functions in Israel's testimony as a delegitimator of failed social institutions and as a legitimator of revolutionary human agents.
>
> . . .
>
> As this tradition stands as a witness and authorization against oppression, it is also a powerful alternative to repression. This tradition is relentlessly public in its orientation, and it resists any psychologizing. Nonetheless, where individual persons find themselves in bondage in more intimate ways, there is no doubt that this same witness to the God who claims these verbs is a powerful force

for *personal* emancipation. As the power of death may take many forms, so also Yahweh's power of life is said to be operative in every dimension of life where issues of liberated existence are at stake.[17]

17. Brueggemann, *Theology of the Old Testament*, 180–81.

4 Revelation in Ancient Context

The simple sequence of statements on horses and chariots (Josh 11:4, 6, 9) is unambiguous. Horses and chariots are a threat to the social experiment that is Israel. Horses and chariots are bad without qualification and unalterably condemned. They symbolize and embody oppression. They function only to impose harsh control on some by others. They must be destroyed. Yahweh authorizes their destruction. Joshua and Israel act in obedience to Yahweh's sovereign command and destroy them. Horses and chariots, according to this narrative, have no positive, useful purpose in the world of ancient Israel, for they serve only to maintain the status quo in which some dominate others. Israel as a liberated community of the Exodus has no need for such a mode of social power.[1] Moreover, Yahweh is the sworn enemy of such modes of power.

Israel's sense of cattle, in this narrative and generally, is very different. Cattle are never instruments of war or oppres-

---

1. It is interesting that in the stylized catalogues of blessings bestowed by God, horses are never listed in such a recital (cf. Job 42:12–16; Deut 11:15; 28:4; Josh 1:14; 2 Kgs 3:17). Whereas cattle belong in such a list, horses regularly are treated as an imposition upon a community by an occupying force, but not as a gift to be treasured in the community. Horses are characteristically threats, not prizes or treasures.

sion. They may be a measure of affluence (Gen 32:15; Jonah 4:11), but they only serve as meat and milk, for domestic and communal well-being. Because they are not symbols of domination and oppression as are horses and chariots, a simple social analysis of cattle is not adequate. In his close reading of Joshua 11, Polzin has discerned a certain playful ambiguity in the narrative concerning cattle and their disposition, an ambiguity that Israel does not have about horses and chariots.[2] Because cattle are not socially unambiguous for Israel as are horses and chariots, Israel's sense of Yahweh's will concerning cattle is also not unambiguous. Horses are clearly for domination. But cattle may be either seductive or sustaining, and so Yahweh's will for their treatment requires more careful, nuanced attention.

We have seen that v. 6 of Joshua 11 gives an unambiguous command on horses and chariots. They are to be destroyed. Concerning cattle and other spoil, however, the narrative departs from the command of v. 6 in two contrasting directions.

1. A total and massive destruction is commanded, a more harsh destruction than that authorized in v. 6:

- *Ḥerem* is practiced, "as Moses the servant of Yahweh had commanded" (v. 12).

- Cattle are taken as spoil, but every man is smote, "as Yahweh had commanded Moses his servant, so Moses commanded Joshua, so Joshua did; he left

2. Polzin, *Moses and the Deuteronomist*, 113–24.

nothing undone of all that Yahweh had commanded Moses" (v. 15).

- *Ḥerem* is practiced again. "It was Yahweh's doing to harden their hearts that they would come against Israel in battle in order that they might be utterly destroyed and might receive no mercy, but be exterminated, as Yahweh's commanded Moses" (v. 20).

- The whole land is seized. "So Joshua took the whole land, according to all that Yahweh had spoken to Moses . . . and the land had rest from war" (v. 23).

Two things are striking about these statements. First, they are not the direct speech of Yahweh, in contrast to v. 6, but are attributed to Moses in a former generation. Yahweh speaks directly about horses and chariots, but only indirectly through Moses about cattle and spoil. The command (and therefore the revelation) is remembered revelation:

- As Moses had commanded (v. 12)
- So Moses commanded Joshua (v. 15).
- Yahweh commanded Moses (v. 20).
- Yahweh had spoken to Moses (v. 23).

Because the revelation is an unspecified reference to older torah, the community of necessity must interpret. Which older torah teaching is invoked is not self-evident, nor exactly how it applies to this situation. This means that with regard to cattle and spoil, there is room for speculation, maneuverability, and alternative decisions.

Second, these mandates that are attributed to Yahweh through the memory of Moses are exceedingly harsh, not as disciplined, specific, and restrained as the command of v. 6:

- to utterly destroy (v. 12)

- not to leave any that breathed (v. 14)

- utterly destroyed, no mercy, exterminated (v. 20)

- took the whole land (v. 23).

In each case an old textual warrant (presumably Deut 20:16–18) is claimed as authorization for the present destruction. That old textual warrant is remembered and presented as uncompromisingly harsh.

2. But in Joshua 11, as Polzin has observed, the command regarding other spoil is also more lenient than the mandate regarding horses and chariots. The command of v. 6 is a harsh command. But as the narrative develops and horses and chariots are to be destroyed, cattle may be taken and saved as booty (v. 14). It is curious that in the very text which urges that "nothing be left breathing," cattle are exempted. The enactment of God's mandate is contextualized by Israel.

The harsh, remembered demand of Moses and the permit of Moses to take spoil (cf. Deut 20:14) both depart from v. 6, the former in a more demanding direction, the latter in a more lenient direction. Both the harshness and the leniency are based on the old torah memory of Deuteronomy 20: in vv. 10–14 and vv. 16–18, respectively. Based on the old torah memory, in the name of Moses our narrative practices both extermination and spoil, both radical rejection of booty and economic prudence, both obedient destruction and self-serving confiscation. Both are warranted by the torah teaching of Deuteronomy 20—a polarity Polzin has not allowed.

I take v. 6, Yahweh's only direct speech in Joshua 11, as the normative revelation within the text. It mandates destruction of a quite specific kind in order to give liberated Israel room to exist. It sanctions neither more nor less than this. In two ways the narrative around v. 6 departs from this normative mandate. On the one hand, in vv. 7–8 Israel did much more than is authorized: "Israel fell . . . smote . . . pursued . . . smote . . . until they left none remaining." They killed people and destroyed cities, surely not decreed by Yahweh in v. 6. On the other hand, one may say they did less, for they took cattle as booty, also not authorized by v. 6. One might construe v. 6 as a directive to immobilize anything held by the hostile city-states, but that is not subsequently understood to include cattle.

The narrative of Joshua 11 thus may be sorted out at three levels:

1. *Theologically*, there is a distinction between what is to be exterminated and what is to be kept as spoil, even though the decree of v. 6 authorizes neither spoil nor extermination. Both extermination and spoil are warranted in the torah tradition of Deuteronomy 20: spoil in vv. 10–14, and extermination in vv. 16–18.[3]

---

3. On the criticism of this text, see Rofé, "The Laws of Warfare in the Book of Deuteronomy."

2. *Sociologically*, there is a distinction between horses (and chariots) and cattle (and other spoil). Horses and cattle symbolize very different things and perform very different social functions. Horses function to dominate because they are a means of military power. Cattle function to sustain by providing meat and milk. Horses can never provide sustenance. Cattle can never aid in oppression.

3. *Methodologically*, there is a distinction between sociological and literary analyses. Thus I have used only sociological methods to ask what horse and chariot symbolize and what social functions they perform and why Yahweh wills their immobilization. To ask a question of the social symbolization and function of horse and chariot leads to something like a "class reading" of the matter, for clearly horse and chariot are tools of domination.

On the other hand (following Polzin), reference to cattle and spoil has evoked subtle literary questions because we are able to see how the tradition struggles with the tension of spoil and extermination, how cattle require a more subtle sorting out than does the socially unambiguous reality of horses. We are able to see that the revelatory operation within the narrative is indeed subtle and requires careful differentiations. Thus horses as tool and symbol of domination permit a clear, unambiguous announcement of God's will. Cattle, which may be a means of seduction (Deut 20:16–18) or a means of sustenance (Deut 20:14–15), require a more delicate articulation of God's will. It will not do simply to ask about "all that violence," because the situation of the text is much more complicated than that. The warrant for violence is grounded in v. 6. One may imagine that Israel took that limited, disciplined warrant of Yahweh and went well beyond its intent or substance in its action, out of rage and oppression.[4] The action against the horses is based on a revelatory permit for liberation. The sanction for keeping cattle looks to the future just community that will replace the oppressive city-states.

What we have, then, is revelation in context. The popular way of putting the question is: Would the God of the Bible mandate such violence? But the question must be posed in context. Of the remembered revelation rooted in the memory of Moses, the answer is yes, in the interest of Israel's survival as a holy people (Deut 7:6). Of the immediate revelation, the answer is yes, as a means of eliminating implements of domination.

But I do not want to evade our governing question: Does God mandate violence? Properly contextualized, this narrative answers yes, but of a specific kind: tightly circumscribed, in the interest of a serious social experiment, in the interest of ending domination. The revelation is not really act, but warrant or permit. The narrative requires us to conclude that this community was utterly persuaded that the God of the tradition is passionately against domination and is passionately for an egalitarian community.

4. On the sociology and power of rage in situations of oppression, see Spina, "The Concept of Social Rage in the Old Testament and the Ancient Near East."

It is futile to try to talk such a community of the oppressed out of such a theological conviction. Its certitude does not arise out of religious rumination, but out of the visceral sense of pain and oppression, which is the stuff of history. This community of Israel, however we articulate its sociology of marginality, knows deep in its bones that God did not intend long-term subservience. Perhaps that conviction came by the bearers of the news of the Exodus,[5] but I suggest it came in their particular context of oppression. The conviction of God's disclosure is linked to that context. Its actual implementation of extermination, hamstringing, and taking spoil is also given in the matrix of social practice, not apart from it. Questions about violence authorized by God must be kept very close to the visceral hurt and hope of such communities of marginality. It is remarkable that the judgment and certitude of such a community has been received by us as canonical, but it has indeed been so received.

The matter of revelation inside the narrative finally requires comment on v. 20:

> For it was Yahweh's doing to harden their hearts that they should come against Israel in battle, in order that they should be utterly destroyed, and might receive no mercy, but be exterminated, just as Yahweh had commanded Moses.

The second half of the verse is controlled by two uses of the Hebrew particle *lema'an* ("in order that"):

5. Gottwald identifies the Levites as the revolutionary cadre who carry this news of the liberation of Yahweh (*The Tribes of Yahweh*, 490–96). Mendenhall, in more "realistic" fashion, urged that the news of exodus was carried specifically by Joshua and Caleb.

> In order that they would come against Israel . . . in
> order that they might be utterly destroyed.

But the intriguing statement is, "It was Yahweh's doing to harden their hearts."[6] What I find interesting about this statement is the question of knowledge: How did Israel know this? How did Israel decide Yahweh did it? The statement does not claim Yahweh was in the battle, but only that Yahweh worked to convene the battle so that there would be a victory. This is a marvelously elusive theological formula to juxtapose to the concreteness of v. 6. God is not immediately involved in any direct way, but Israel knows that governance is finally in Yahweh's hands as was the case in the remembered Exodus (Exod 4:21; 7:3; 9:12; 10:1). The conclusion drawn in v. 20 asserts the majestic, irresistible sovereignty of Yahweh. But that grand claim of sovereignty finally rests on the concreteness of v. 6. Without the concreteness of v. 6, the claim of v. 20 is without substance.

---

6. On the problematic of this theological theme, see von Rad, *Old Testament Theology*, 2:151–55; Childs, *The Book of Exodus*, 170–75; and Wilson, "The Hardening of Pharaoh's Heart."

5 *Revelation and Canonical Reading*

Now we may turn to the second question of revelation, the disclosure given by the narrative as narrative, not to its own participants, but to us who now stand outside the narrative, take it as canonical, and heed it as revelatory. A good test is to ask: What would we know of the ways and character of God if we had only this particular rendering? Or what would be lost if we did not have this text?

I have proposed that Yahweh's command in Joshua 11:6 is theologically normative. It is not as harsh as general extermination. It is not as lenient as taking spoil. This theologically normative disclosure concerns Yahweh's hostility to horses and chariots, which are monarchic instruments of domination.[1] These instruments of domination:

- require advanced technology

- require surplus wealth to finance and maintain, and

- serve a political, economic monopoly dependent on oppression and subservience.

---

1. Boling and Wright, *Joshua*, 307, conclude, "Such military efficiency reflects a feudal system in which the charioteers, or *maryanu*, belong to a class enjoying special privileges and performing special services for the king." Gottwald, *Tribes of Yahweh*, 543, writes, "Hamstringing horses and burning chariots were defensive measures against the hated and feared superior weaponry of the enemy."

We have ample evidence to suggest the social function of horses and chariots for kings. In the inventory of Solomon's affluence and security, he is said to have forty thousand stalls of horses for his chariots and twelve thousand horsemen (1 Kgs 4:26). In 1 Kings 10:26 it is reported "Solomon gathered together chariots and horses; he had fourteen hundred chariots and twelve thousand horsemen," partly for trade, but mostly for defense and intimidation.[2] The Bible characteristically associates horses and chariots with royal power, which is regularly seen to be oppressive (cf. Exod 14:9, 23; Deut 20:1; 2 Sam 15:1; 1 Kgs 18:5; 22:4; 2 Kgs 3:7; 18:23; 23:11).

Yahweh's hostility to horses and chariots bespeaks Yahweh's hostility to the social system that requires, legitimates, and depends upon them. Israel, in its early period of tribal-peasant life, did not have horses and chariots and greatly feared them. The struggle reflected in Joshua 11 is how this community, so vulnerable and helpless, can exist and function against the kings and their powerful tools of domination.

In light of the inventory of the royal use of horses and chariots, we now consider an alternative set of texts expressed in a very different mode that present a critical view of horses and chariots. These narrative accounts are in a sense expository comments on the sanction of Joshua 11:6.

The Bible is not content simply to describe the royal status quo, which seems beyond challenge. The Bible also offers

2. Clearly Solomon's monarchy embodies much that repelled the Israel of Moses and Joshua. See Mendenhall, "The Monarchy."

tales of liberation that show Israel challenging, countering, and overcoming this formidable royal power. The narrative form lends itself to the articulation of another kind of power that the royal world neither knows nor credits.[3] The narrative mode challenges royal rationality even as the narrative substance challenges royal policy.

1. In 1 Kings 20, Israel is ranged against Aram (Syria) in an uneven contest. The Arameans (Syrians), a prototype of military power, are sure of their strength:

> The servants of the king of Aram said to him, "Their gods are gods of the hills, and so they were stronger than we; but let us fight against them in the plain, and surely we shall be stronger than they . . . And muster an army like the army that you have lost, horse for horse, and chariot for chariot; then we will fight against them in the plain, and surely we will be stronger than they." (20:23–25)

The Israelites, in their own narrative presentation, are helpless by contrast:

> And the people of Israel encamped before them like two little flocks of goats, but the Arameans filled the country. (20:27)

3. The different sociology of these texts needs to be correlated with the different mode of literary expression in which it is reported. Thus the positive assertion of royal power is characteristically reported in lists, inventories, and memos. By contrast, the alternative power of Yahweh does not come articulated in such controlled modes of expression, but in narratives of a playful kind, which allow for surprise and inscrutability. The modes of power are matched to ways of speech and to the different epistemologies and rationalities practiced by the speech forms.

The narrative makes the disproportion of royal power clear. That in turn makes the victory of Yahweh all the more dramatic:

> Because the Arameans have said, "Yahweh is a god of the hills, but he is not a god of the valleys," therefore I will give all this great multitude into your hand, and you shall know that I am Yahweh. (20:28)

The episode concludes with a great victory. Israel's God and Israel's narrators are undaunted by the odds of royal horses and chariots. They are undaunted because there is another power that overwhelms and overrides the royal establishment and gives victory to these seemingly helpless peasants.

Notice that at the crucial point of the narrative where we would want specificity, we are told nothing.[4] At the point where we would like to know how Yahweh defeated the Syrian horses and chariots, the narrative is opaque. We are not told. It is enough to receive the surprising news that is against the data. It is enough to know that Yahweh triumphs over the Syrian gods, and therefore Israel triumphs over Syria, and therefore faith triumphs over horses and chariots.

2. A second narrative that offers a critique of horses and chariots again concerns Syria, Israel, and Elisha (2 Kgs 6:15–19). Syria discerns that Elisha is the main threat and sends "horses

---

4. The formula "I will give" is characteristically the way of victory, as we have seen it also in Joshua 11:6. On the formula, see the comment of von Rad, *Holy War in Ancient Israel*, 42–44. The phrase promises everything but tells nothing.

and chariots and a great army" to seize him (2 Kgs 6:14). Yahweh's prophet is in great danger and seemingly defenseless. But the narrative focuses on the faith of Elisha and the power of Yahweh.

First, Elisha issues a formal assurance: "Fear not, for those who are with us are more than those who are with them" (v. 16).[5] Second, Elisha prays that frightened Israel, embodied in his servant, may see (v. 17). And third, in answer to the prayer, Yahweh causes the young man to see: "And behold, the mountain was full of horses and chariots of fire round about Elisha" (v. 17). Again the narrative is elliptical just at the place where we would like to know more. It is enough for our purposes, however, to see that through the prophetic person, the power of prayer, and the courage of faith, Yahweh's powerful sovereignty is present in horses and chariots that effectively counter the Syrians (v. 17).

3. In a different episode of this same extended narrative, the motif of Yahweh's defeat of horses and chariots recurs (2 Kgs 7:3–8). Four lepers enter the camp of the Syrians, but the Syrians had all fled. Persons as socially irrelevant as lepers can safely enter the Syrian stronghold.

The narrative explanation for the flight of the Syrians is this:

> For Yahweh had made the army of the Arameans
> hear the sound of chariots and horses, the sound
> of a great army, so that they said to one another,

5. The formula is the same as in Joshua 11:6.

> "Behold, the king of Israel has hired against us the kings of the Hittites and the kings of Egypt to come upon us." So they fled away in the twilight and forsook their tents, their horses and their asses, leaving the camp as it was, and fled for their lives. (2 Kgs 7:6–7)

The narrative continues, saying that the lepers seized spoil of silver, gold, and clothing (v. 8).[6] Again a victory is inscrutably won by Yahweh against the great odds of the military power of a foreign state. The mode of the victory is comic, whimsical, or hidden. But it is decisive. The Israelites had not hired allies as Syria suspected (v. 6). Israel did not need allies other than Yahweh. The narrator understands this perfectly, but the marching Syrians have no access to the reality evoked by this narrative. The narrative thus delegitimates the rationality of Syrian royal power.

The outcome of all three narratives in 1 Kings 20 and 2 Kings 6 and 7 is that Yahweh is shown to be stronger than the military state and is its sworn enemy on behalf of Yahweh's own people. Generation after generation, the strange turn of the Exodus is reenacted with new characters, but each time on behalf of helpless Israel. The narratives do not tell us all we would like to know about the course of the battles. But they tell us all Israel needs to know about Yahweh, which is that Yahweh is faithful, is sovereign, and will not be mocked.

The mode of the power of Yahweh is prophetic speech. The prophets mobilize that power against the state. The states

6. The seizure of spoil from the strong ones now defeated by Yahweh is parallel to Joshua 11.

may have asked cynically, "How many legions does Elisha have?" But against such cynicism toward Yahweh, the narrative answers, "Enough." It is not royal horses and chariots, but the power of Yahweh that ultimately shapes the outcome of the historical process. Clearly we are dealing here with a very different rationality, a rationality that refuses to accommodate royal reason. The narratives have no great attraction to violence, but they also are not embarrassed by what is necessary for survival and well-being.

4. In one other narrative, we note the cynicism of the Assyrians who mock Israelite weakness by an offer of two thousand horses if Israel has riders to mount, which obviously Israel does not (2 Kgs 18:24). The imperial speaker taunts Israel for depending on Egyptian horses and chariots. But the taunt is defeated, for Yahweh takes the challenge and overcomes the Assyrian threat.

In all these liberation narratives, royal monopoly of power is countered. It is countered by the prophecy that discloses unseen and unrecognized horses and chariots (2 Kgs 6:16–17). It is countered in 2 Kings 7:6 by the sound of horses and chariots, created by Yahweh. It is countered in 1 Kings 20:28 when Yahweh hands over the Syrians. It is countered by the powerful angel of Yahweh (2 Kgs 19:35). In all these texts, the narrative reveals Yahweh's power, which inscrutably and effectively counters hostile, oppressive royal power. The narrative shows Syrian horses and chariots not to be as powerful as was assumed. Israel and the Syrians are permitted to see what they had not seen. And for us, the narrative asserts the reality of Yahweh in modes for which we are not prepared.

In our consideration of revelation and violence, we have juxtaposed two contrasting kinds of material. On the one hand, we have mentioned rather flat, descriptive accounts of royal power (Exod 14:9, 23; Deut 20:1; 2 Sam 15:1; 1 Kgs 18:5; 22:4; 2 Kgs 3:7; 18:23; 23:11). These texts read like official memos and sound in their rendering like the cool, detached reasoning of technique, perhaps resembling the congressional testimony of Secretary of Defense Donald Rumsfeld during the run-up to war with Iraq, in which everything is obvious, acceptable, reasonable, taken for granted, and not to be questioned. Such a mode of evidence is hardly revelatory, for it discloses nothing. It only states once again the already known.

By contrast, the narratives we have considered disclose what was not known. The narrative of 1 Kings 20:26–30 shows Israel, which seemed to be "like two little flocks of goats," to be empowered by Yahweh's response to the mocking, and therefore available for a victory. In 2 Kings 6:16–17, reality is evoked by a prophetic pronouncement of "fear not," which ends in an unexpected vision of horses and chariots of Yahweh, who seemed to have none. In 2 Kings 7:16, it is the very sound of horses and chariots that frightened the Syrians. In 2 Kings 19:35, an angel of Yahweh repels the imperial army. All four stories offer a different mode of presentation, a different epistemology, and a different universe of discourse. This is narrative art that invites to bold, imaginative faith a community that is short on royal technique. But this community is not without its own peculiar rationality that believes that the world is ordered, governed, and powered by an authority to which kings do not have access and over which they cannot prevail. The narratives reveal that faithful imagination is more powerful than dominating technique. The narratives offer a convergence of:

- *narrative primitivism,*
  which is obligated to explain nothing;

- *social marginality,*
  which cannot rely on human resources;

- *epistemological naïveté,*
  which refuses royal modes of certitude; and

- *theological amazement,*
  which is innocent and desperate enough to believe, and is not disappointed.

These factors together in the four narratives of 1 Kings 20:26–30; 2 Kings 6:16–17; 7:16; and 18:19—19:37 are indeed revelatory. They disclose what had not been seen. They make known what had not been known. And when this alternative is known and seen, the sure, managed world of royal technique and certitude is stunningly dismantled. The rulers of this age are marvelously put to flight. Israel's life is rendered in these narratives in an alternative rationality that has power, substance, and reality, all rooted in and derived from this subversive disclosure of Yahweh.

Yahweh's inscrutable competence against royal horses and chariots is echoed in the odd prayer and teaching of Jesus:

> "I thank you, Father, Lord of heaven and earth, because you have hidden these things from the wise and the intelligent and revealed them to infants; yes, Father, for such was your gracious will." . . . Then turning to the disciples he said privately: "Blessed are the eyes which see what you see! For I tell you that many prophets and kings desired to see what you see, and did not see it, and to hear what you hear, and did not hear it." (Luke 10:21–24)[7]

What is hidden from the kings is disclosed to the prophets in Israel. They see and know another kind of power.

We have observed texts that, in a descriptive way, document the inventory of royal chariots. These texts we take either as factual reports or as polemics against royal power. Second, we have observed texts that tell tales of alternative forms of power that triumph over royal instruments of domination. The contrast between the descriptions of royal domination and narratives of alternative forms of power reflects Israel's alternative reading of the historical process. The mode of expression that contrasts flat description and imaginative narrative corresponds to the modes of power that may be discerned in the historical process. In ancient Israel, the imaginative narrative is characteristically stronger than the

---

7. On the peculiar character of this saying, see Suggs, *Wisdom, Christology and Law in St. Matthew's Gospel*, 71–97.

descriptive memo. The narrative more nearly articulates the decisive direction of the historical process. That is, the mode of discourse correlates with ways of reality and modes of power. How Israel speaks is related to what Israel trusts in and hopes for.[8]

That contrast between descriptive inventory and imaginative narrative leads to a warning that Israel should not imitate or be seduced by such royal modes of power (cf. Deut 17:14–20)[9] or royal modes of communication.[10] If Israel imitates the foreign kingdoms or is seduced by their power or their gods, Israel will also become an agent of domination.

The seductive economics of Solomon goes along with the changed modes of communication. In contrast to David, it is telling that we have no narratives of Solomon in the sense that we have them about David. One may say that Solomon got horses and chariots and lost narrative. I suggest we will not understand what is at issue in our present society of militarism until we see the connection between modes of power and modes of speech.

8. O'Day, *Revelation in the Fourth Gospel*, has shown that the *Wie* ("how") of presentation is as important as *Dass* ("that") and *Was* ("what") for understanding this literature as revelatory.

9. The basis of *herem* is not that Israel should not possess, but that Israel should not be seduced. I am not sure if Polzin has recognized this difference.

10. On the seduction of royal modes of communication, the substantive issue is the loss of narrative, embarrassment over storytelling, and the recasting of reality into technical modes of communication. On this general seduction and its social outcome, see Frei, *The Eclipse of Biblical Narrative*.

Israel knows it is not to emulate royal modes of power, knowledge, or language. Israel also knows that alternative modes of power, knowledge, and language are available that permit freedom and justice.

6 *Yahweh versus Horse and Chariot*

Our study has considered in turn:

- descriptive inventories of royal domination through horses and chariots,

- imaginative narratives of alternative power concerning Yahweh's power against horses and chariots,

- prohibition against imitation and seduction by such horses and chariots.

Israel developed an important and sustained theological tradition that affirmed that the power of Yahweh is stronger than the royal power of horses and chariots. In all parts of the biblical tradition, it is affirmed that the power of Yahweh will defeat oppressive kings who have horses and chariots. The "power of Yahweh" is not explained in detail. Obviously the power of Yahweh belongs to a very different, nonroyal rationality; but the tradition does not doubt that the power is effective in actual, concrete, historical interactions.[1]

---

1. On the power of Yahweh articulated as "the hand of Yahweh," see P. D. Miller and Roberts, *The Hand of the Lord*.

The motif of Yahweh's triumph over horses and chariots may be found in three kinds of texts, which range over the entire Old Testament literature.

PROPHETIC TEXTS

Prophetic texts assert the liberating power of God over against royal domination:

> I will have pity on the house of Judah,
>> and I will deliver them by Yahweh their God;
> I will not deliver them by bow or by sword,
>> or by war, or by horses, or by horsemen. (Hos 1:7)[2]

> Alas to those who go down to Egypt for help,
>> and who rely on horses,
> who trust in chariots because they are many
>> and in horsemen because they are very strong,
> but do not look to the Holy One of Israel
>> or consult Yahweh. (Isa 31:1, cf. v. 3; and 30:15–16)[3]

> In the day, says Yahweh,
>> I will cut off your horses from among you
>> and I will destroy your chariots. (Mic 5:10)[4]

2. On this verse, see Wolff, *Hosea*, 20–21.

3. On the issue of faith in Isaiah, see von Rad, *Old Testament Theology*, 2:158–69. An investigation of the term *baṭaḥ* in the tradition of Isaiah would be worth pursuing; see Jepsen, "בטח."

4. One can understand the polemic of the Micah tradition if one accepts the sociological analysis of Wolff that Micah is the voice of the small rural landowner always resistant to imperial impingement. Cf.

The text of Micah goes on to speak of destroying cities, sorceries and images:

> And in the anger and wrath will I execute vengeance
>   on the nations that did not obey. (Mic 5:15)

> Thus says Yahweh,
>   who makes a way in the sea,
>   a path in the mighty waters,
> who brings forth chariot and horse,
>   army and warrior,
> they lie down, they cannot rise,
>   they are extinguished, quenched like a wick.
>   (Isa 43:16–17)

This reference alludes to the Exodus and is followed by the remarkable assertion, "Behold, I am doing a new thing," i.e., Yahweh is crushing the horses and chariots of Babylon and so permitting exiled Israel to go home.

> This is the word of Yahweh to Zerubbabel: not by
> might, nor by power, but by my spirit, says Yahweh
> of hosts. (Zech 4:6)

To be sure, in this well-known text, horses and chariots are not mentioned; but I consider this statement to be an extension of the same trajectory. Yahweh's opposition to royal, military power is in this text couched in apocalyptic language. But the claim of Yahweh's governance is the same. Prophetic faith sets

---

Wolff, "Micah the Moreshite—The Prophet and His Background"; and *Micah the Prophet*. Hillers, *Micah*, 72–74, interprets Micah's prophecy as a renunciation of all that destroys Israel's true identity.

the inscrutable power of Yahweh over against the pretensions of state power. This paradigmatic antithesis is acted out already in the Exodus narrative.[5]

PSALMS

In the Psalms, the motif of horses and chariots is articulated:

> Some boast in chariots, and some of horses,
>> but we boast in the name of Yahweh our God.
>
> (Ps 20:7)

In this royal psalm, the contrast between conventional royal power and the power of Yahweh is total. The verb "boast" here is a rendering of *zakar* and so should not be overinterpreted.[6] But the conventional rendering "boast" suggests a proximity to Jeremiah 9:23–24 (which in turn is quoted in 1 Corinthians 1:31).[7]

5. The contrast between the power of Yahweh and the pretensions of state power is nicely drawn in 1 Samuel 17:45 and the encompassing narrative. See my discussion in *David's Truth*, in which I have drawn attention to the epistemology of the tribe that is articulated to claim a zone of freedom against a hostile state.

6. The use of the term *zakar* here is peculiar. Its conventional rendering of "boast" is surely correct, but perhaps it also linked the present doxology to concrete memories of the triumphs of Yahweh in the past, which were won against great odds. It is the memory that permits the doxology.

7. The verb in Jeremiah 9:22–23 is *halal*. On the text from Jeremiah, see Brueggemann, "The Epistemological Crisis of Israel's Two Histories (Jer. 9:22–23)."

A king is not saved by his great army,
> a warrior is not delivered by his great strength.

The war horse is a vain hope for victory,
> and by its great strength it cannot save. (Ps 33:16–17)

At your rebuke, O God of Jacob,
> both rider and horse lay stunned

But indeed are awesome! (Ps 76:6–7a)

His delight is not in the strength of the horse
> nor his pleasure in the speed of a runner;

but Yahweh takes pleasure[8] in those who fear him,
> in those who hope in his steadfast love.
>
> (Ps 147:10–11)

PROVERBS

The question of what constitutes power also appears in Proverbs:

> No wisdom, no understanding, no counsel
>> can avail against Yahweh.
>
> The horse is made ready for the day of battle,
>> but victory belongs to Yahweh. (Prov 21:30–31)

Von Rad has identified this text along with five others that articulate the hidden, inscrutable ways of Yahweh's gover-

---

8. The verb *ḥapaṣ* used here is the same as in Jeremiah 9:23.

nance that challenge all human self-security, whether by way of knowledge, power, planning, or ingenuity.[9]

CONCLUSION

In all these texts—prophetic assertions (Hos 1:7; Isa 31:1; Mic 5:10; Isa 43:15–17; Zech 4:6), psalmic doxologies (Pss 20:7; 33:16–17; 76:6–7; 147:10–11), and sapiential discernment (Prov 21:30–31)—we have theological statements that are eloquent and not problematic. In the texts, the difficult issue of Yahweh's involvement in violence is not visible. Yet all these texts are rooted in and derived from the much more primitive statement of Joshua 11:6: "hamstring the horses and burn the chariots." The other more removed statements depend on the concreteness of such a warrant. Yahweh's sovereignty over horses and chariots is made visible in that concrete action which Yahweh authorizes.

9. Von Rad, *Old Testament Theology* 1:438–41; and *Wisdom in Israel*, 97–110.

7 *Despite Chariots of Iron*

The theological outcome of Joshua 11 concerns the will and capacity of Yahweh to overturn the present historical arrangements of society that are judged to be inequitable and against the purposes of Yahweh. Yahweh is here revealed as the true governor of the historical-political process, armed alternatives notwithstanding. At the beginning of the narrative, Israel is assaulted by superior force (Josh 11:1). But by word (v. 6) and by inscrutable, hidden intervention (v. 20), Israel receives its inheritance and rest according to God's promise (v. 23). Yahweh is disclosed as a God who keeps promises within the historical arena. The narrative is a tale of a transformation from domination to inheritance wrought by Yahweh's sovereign will through Israel's bold obedience.

Two texts may be cited that marvelously articulate this strange narrative faith that creates social possibility against a new might. First, at the decisive pause in the land narrative, this encounter takes place. The tribes of Ephraim and Manasseh articulate their weakness in the face of Canaanite chariots:

> The hill country is not enough for us; yet all the
> Canaanites who dwell in the plain have chariots of

> iron, both those in Beth-shean and its villages and
> those in the Valley of Jezreel. (Josh 17:16)

Joshua, man of faith, responds with an assurance:

> Then Joshua said to the house of Joseph, to Ephraim
> and Manasseh, "You are a numerous people, and
> have great power; you shall not have one lot only,
> but the hill country shall be yours, for though it is
> a forest, you shall clear it and possess it to its far-
> thest borders; you shall drive out the Canaanites,
> though they have chariots of iron, and though they
> are strong." (17:17–18)

It is this summons to faith that makes the difference. The
voice of hope is the great equalizer in the historical process.

Second, at the deathbed scene of Elisha (who had con-
siderable experience against horses and chariots), King Joash
grieves, because without this prophetic voice of hope he
knows he is hopeless and helpless. The king laments:

> My father, my father. The chariots of Israel and its
> horsemen. (2 Kgs 13:14; cf. 2:12)

The king acknowledges that the prophetic figure of Elisha is
Israel's mode of power in the world, the only resource this
community has in a world of harsh power.

I conclude with four comments:

1. The fundamental claim of Joshua 11 is that Yahweh is disclosed as a God who will invert the historical process and
give land to the landless. That claim, so far as the tradition is
concerned, is beyond dispute. The command against horses
and chariots looks back to the defeat of Pharaoh in Exodus

(14:6–7, 23; cf. Exod 15:1, 21) and Sisera (Judg 4:3, 7, 13–16),[1] and forward to the defeat of Babylon (Isa 43:16–21)—all texts concerning horses and chariots and imperial power. The troublesome part is that Yahweh's transforming governance takes place in such concrete, human ways as hamstringing and burning. Everything hinges on this warrant for action; the faithful act of obedience, so featured in Joshua 11, is response to the permit of Yahweh. In biblical faith the great gift of deliverance comes in historical concreteness.

2. For the people in the text, we ask: Is this really revelation? Does God say such things as in Joshua 11:6? When the permit of Yahweh is embedded in this community of marginality, when revelation is taken as the community's sense of its future with God, this is indeed a disclosure, for it must be so if this community is to have a genuine historical future. None in the community doubted either that God willed such a future, or that the future came at great risk.

3. If revelation is to be always embedded in context, then we must see if this narrative of Joshua is disclosure from God for communities of marginality in our own time that face the great odds of horses and chariots. The affirmation of third-world communities of faith is that God's great promise of land and justice is indeed linked to concrete human

---

1. Gottwald has established a model of interpretation that takes Moses and Joshua together. He has treated as continuous the Egyptian empire and the Canaanite city-state as metaphors of oppression. In Joshua 4:23, it is evident that the cultic tradition labored to establish the same equation.

acts against horses and chariots. As in ancient peasant Israel, none can persuade such communities of faith and hope that the God of justice and freedom withholds such a permit. As Gerstenberger puts it:

> It seems to me that by virtue of all that we can think to be theologically correct in our pluralistic world, which is everywhere struggling for its survival, the exploited groups or societies whose downfall has been brought about by the ruling powers must be accorded a legitimate right to defence and resistance—in extreme cases even extending to armed struggle. That the resistance of the oppressed often turns into a terror that has contempt for human beings is the other side of the coin. The theologically legitimate battle for liberation lies on a narrow path which runs between abysses. But there is this way.[2]

4. In our own cultural context, however, we must read the narrative as disclosure "from the other side" within communities of domination. We are more fully embedded in communities of horses and chariots, more fully committed to domination. The narrative and its trajectory as I have traced it suggest that such communities of domination have no warrant for arms and control, but that this God in inscrutable ways is aligned against the horses and chariots, working through hardness of heart, until the whole enterprise collapses. The powerful lineage of Pharaoh, Sisera, Nebuchadnezzar never learns in time. But the text persists and is always offered again. It is a disclosure of hope to those embedded in reliance on horses and

---

2. Gerstenberger, *Theologies in the Old Testament*, 157.

chariots, a warning that all such arms cannot secure against God's force for life. This partisan, contextualized disclosure does not regard hamstringing and burning as unacceptable violence. Rather, the disclosure is aimed against domination by the Canaanite. It is maddening that at the crucial places, the text mumbles about how the power of Yahweh could work against such hardware and such technique. But the text, where it mumbles, mumbles because the power of the Spirit cannot be articulated in the rationality of the kings. Indeed, perhaps what is finally disclosed is that the power of God, the rush of the Spirit toward liberation, will never be articulated in the rationality of domination.

From that awareness it is not a very large step to claim that,

> The foolishness of God is wiser than humanity,
>> and the weakness of God is stronger than humanity.
>
> (1 Cor 1:25)

That insight is already celebrated in Joshua 11, where these land-desperate people watched while the powerful city-kings were undone by the command, permit, and warrant of Yahweh. The rhetoric of such a narrative is not congenial to us in our royal rationality. It is precisely emancipation from that royal rationality, however, that lets another mode of speech render another mode of life, wrought by a very different kind of power.

Bibliography

Alt, Albrecht. "Josua." In *Kleine Schriften zur Geschichte des Volkes Israel*, 1:176–92. Munich: Beck, 1953.

Alter, Robert. *The Art of Biblical Narrative*. New York: Basic Books, 1981.

Barton, John. *Reading the Old Testament: Method in Biblical Study*. Rev. ed. Philadelphia: Westminster, 1996.

Bergant, Dianne. "Peace in a Universe of Order." In *Biblical and Theological Reflections on "The Challenge of Peace,"* edited by John T. Pawlikowski and Donald Senior, 17–30. Wilmington, DE: Glazier, 1984.

Berger, Peter, and Thomas Luckmann. *The Social Construction of Reality: A Treatise on the Sociology of Knowledge*. Garden City, NY: Doubleday, 1966.

Berne, Eric. *Beyond Games and Scripts*. New York: Ballantine, 1976.

———. *What Do You Say After You Say Hello?* New York: Bantam, 1972.

Berquist, Jon L. *Judaism in Persia's Shadow: A Social and Historical Approach*. 1995. Reprinted, Eugene, OR: Wipf & Stock, 2003.

Boff, Leonardo. *Church: Charisma and Power*. New York: Crossroad, 1985.

Boling, Robert G. "Joshua, Book of." In *The Anchor Bible Dictionary*, edited by David Noel Freedman, 3:1002–15. New York: Doubleday, 1992.

———, and G. Ernest Wright. *Joshua*. Anchor Bible 6. Garden City, NY: Doubleday, 1982.

Brueggemann, Walter. "Always in the Shadow of Empire." In *Texts that Linger, Words that Explode*, edited by Patrick D. Miller, 73–87. Minneapolis: Fortress, 2000.

———. "As the Text 'Makes Sense.'" *The Christian Ministry* 14 (Nov 1983) 7–10.

———. *David's Truth in Israel's Imagination and Memory*. 2nd ed. Minneapolis: Fortress, 2002.

———. "The Epistemological Crisis of Israel's Two Histories (Jer. 9:22–23)." In *Israelite Wisdom: Theological and Literary Essays in Honor of Samuel Terrien*, edited by John G. Gammie, 85–105. Missoula, MT: Scholars, 1978. Reprinted in *Old Testament Theology: Essays on Structure, Theme, and Text*, edited by Patrick D. Miller, 270–95.

———. *Hope within History*. Atlanta: John Knox, 1987.

———. *Old Testament Theology: Essays on Structure, Theme, and Text*. Edited by Patrick D. Miller. Minneapolis: Fortress, 1992.

———. *A Pathway of Interpretation: The Old Testament for Pastors and Students*. Eugene, OR: Cascade Books, 2008.

———. "The Prophetic Word of God." In *Texts that Linger, Words that Explode*, edited by Patrick D. Miller, 35–44. Minneapolis: Fortress, 2000.

———. *Solomon: Israel's Ironic Icon of Human Achievement*. Studies on Personalities of the Old Testament. Columbia: University of South Carolina Press, 2005.

———. *Texts under Negotiation: The Bible and Postmodern Imagination*. Minneapolis: Fortress, 1993.

———. *Theology of the Old Testament: Testimony, Dispute, Advocacy*. Minneapolis: Fortress, 1997.

Butler, Trent C. *Joshua*. Word Biblical Commentary 7. Waco: Word, 1983.

Carter, Charles. "Social Scientific Approaches." In *Blackwell Companion to the Hebrew Bible*, edited by Leo G. Perdue, 36–58. Malden, MA: Blackwell, 2001.

Chaney, Marvin L. "Systemic Study of the Israelite Monarchy." *Semeia* 37 (1986) 53–76.

Childs, Brevard S. *The Book of Exodus*. Old Testament Library. Philadelphia: Westminster, 1974.

———. *Introduction to the Old Testament as Scripture*. Philadelphia: Fortress, 1979.

Clevenot, Michel. *Materialist Approaches to the Bible*. Maryknoll, NY: Orbis, 1985.

Clines, David J. A. *I, He, We and They: A Literary Approach to Isaiah 53*. Journal for the Study of the Old Testament: Supplement Series 1. Sheffield: Department of Biblical Studies, University of Sheffield, 1976.

Collins, John J. *Does the Bible Justify Violence?* Facets. Minneapolis: Fortress, 2004.

———. *Introduction to the Hebrew Bible*. Minneapolis: Fortress, 2004.

Conrad, Edgar W. "The 'Fear Not' Oracles in Second Isaiah." *Vetus Testamentum* 34 (1984) 129–52.

———. *Fear Not Warrior: A Study of the 'al tira' Pericopes in the Hebrew Scriptures*. Brown Judaic Studies 75. Chico, CA: Scholars, 1985.

Coote, Robert B. "The Book of Joshua." In *New Interpreter's Bible,* 2:553–719. Nashville: Abingdon, 1998.

Craigie, Peter C. *The Problem of War in the Old Testament*. Grand Rapids: Eerdmans, 1978.

Crossan, John Dominic, editor. *Paul Ricoeur on Biblical Hermeneutics. Semeia* 4 (1975).

Dorr, Donal. *Spirituality and Justice*. Maryknoll, NY: Orbis, 1984.

Flanagan, James. *David's Social Drama: A Hologram of Israel's Early Iron Age*. Journal for the Study of the Old Testament: Supplement Series 73. Sheffield: Almond, 1988.

Frei, Hans. *The Eclipse of Biblical Narrative: A Study in Eighteenth and Nineteenth Century Hermeneutics*. New Haven: Yale University Press, 1974.

Füssel, Kuno. "The Materialist Reading of the Bible." In *The Bible and Liberation*, edited by Norman K. Gottwald, 134–46. Maryknoll, NY: Orbis, 1983.

Geertz, Clifford. "Ideology as a Cultural System." In *The Interpretation of Cultures*, 193–233. New York: Basic Books, 1973.

Gerstenberger, Erhard S. *Theologies in the Old Testament*. Translated by John Bowden. Minneapolis: Fortress, 2002.

Gilkey, Langdon. "Cosmology, Ontology, and the Travail of Biblical Language." *Journal of Religion* 41 (1961) 194–205.

Good, Robert M. "The Just War in Ancient Israel." *Journal of Biblical Literature* 104 (1985) 385–400.

Gottwald, Norman K. *The Hebrew Bible: A Socio-literary Introduction*. Philadelphia: Fortress, 1985.

———. *The Hebrew Bible in Its Social World and in Ours*. Semeia Studies. Atlanta: Scholars, 1993.

———. "Social History of the United Monarchy: An Application of H. A. Landsberger's Framework for the Analysis of Peasant Movements to the Participation of Free Agrarians in the Introduction of the Monarchy to Ancient Israel." Paper read to the SBI, Seminar on Sociology of the "Monarchy," 1983.

———. *The Tribes of Yahweh: A Sociology of the Religion of Liberated Israel, 1250–1050 B.C.E.* Maryknoll, NY: Orbis, 1979.

Grabbe, Lester L. *Priests, Prophets, Diviners, Sages: A Socio-historical Study of Religious Specialists in Ancient Israel*. Valley Forge, PA: Trinity, 1995.

Grant, Brian W. *Schizophrenia: A Source of Social Insight*. Philadelphia: Westminster, 1975.

Gray, John. *Joshua, Judges, and Ruth*. 2nd ed. New Century Bible. Grand Rapids: Eerdmans, 1986.

Gunn, David M. *The Fate of King Saul: An Interpretation of a Biblical Story*. Journal for the Study of the Old Testament Supplement Series 14. Sheffield: Department of Biblical Studies, University of Sheffield, 1980.

———. "Joshua and Judges." In *The Literary Guide to the Bible*, edited by Robert Alter and Frank Kermode, 102–21. Cambridge: Belknap, 1987.

———. *The Story of King David: Genre and Interpretation*. Journal for the Study of the Old Testament Supplement Series 6. Sheffield: Department of Biblical Studies, University of Sheffield, 1978.

Habermas, Jürgen. *Knowledge and Human Interests*. Translated by Jeremy J. Shapiro. Boston: Beacon, 1971.

Hanson, K. C., and Douglas E. Oakman. *Palestine in the Time of Jesus: Social Structures and Social Conflicts*. 2nd ed. Minneapolis: Fortress, 2008.

Hanson, Paul D. *The Dawn of Apocalyptic: The Historical and Sociological Roots of Apocalyptic Eschatology*. Rev. ed. Philadelphia: Fortress, 1979.

———. "War and Peace in the Hebrew Bible." *Interpretation* 38 (1984) 341–62.

Hauerwas, Stanley. *Against the Nations: War and Survival in a Liberal Society*. Minneapolis: Winston, 1985.

―――. *Should War Be Eliminated? Philosophical and Theological Investigations*. Milwaukee: Marquette University Press, 1984.

Hillers, Delbert R. *Micah*. Hermeneia. Philadelphia: Fortress, 1984.

Hobbs, T. R. *A Time for War: A Study of Warfare in the Old Testament*. Old Testament Studies 3. Wilmington, DE: Glazier, 1989.

Jepsen, Alfred. "בטח." In *Theological Dictionary of the Old Testament*, edited by G. Johannes Botterweck and Helmer Ringgren, 2:88–94. Translated by John T. Willis. Rev. ed. Grand Rapids: Eerdmans, 1975.

Jobling, David. *The Sense of Biblical Narrative: Structural Analyses in the Hebrew Bible*. 2nd ed. Journal for the Study of the Old Testament Supplement Series 7. Sheffield: Department of Biblical Studies, University of Sheffield, 1986.

Jones, G. H. "The Concept of Holy War." In *The World of Ancient Israel: Sociological, Anthropological and Political Perspectives*, edited by R. E. Clements, 299–321. Cambridge: Cambridge University Press, 1989.

Kang, Sa-Moon. *Divine War in the Old Testament and in the Ancient Near East*. BZAW 177. Berlin: Töpelmann, 1989.

Kaufman, Gordon D. "On the Meaning of 'Act of God.'" *Harvard Theological Review* 61 (1968) 175–201.

Kautsky, John. *The Politics of Aristocratic Empires*. Chapel Hill: University of North Carolina Press, 1982.

Kegan, Robert. *The Evolving Self: Problem and Process in Human Development*. Cambridge: Harvard University Press, 1982.

Kelsey, David H. *The Uses of Scripture in Recent Theology*. Philadelphia: Fortress, 1975.

Kermode, Frank. *The Art of Telling: Essays on Fiction*. Cambridge: Harvard University Press, 1983.

Lenski, Gerhard. *Power and Privilege: A Theory of Social Stratification*. 2nd ed. Chapel Hill: University of North Carolina Press, 1984.

McKenzie, John L. "The Social Character of Inspiration." *Catholic Biblical Quarterly* 24 (1962) 115–24.

Mendenhall, George E. "The Hebrew Conquest of Palestine." *Biblical Archaeologist Reader* 3 (1970) 100–120.

———. "The Monarchy." *Interpretation* 29 (1975) 155–70.

Meyers, Carol. *Discovering Eve: Ancient Israelite Women in Context.* Oxford: Oxford University Press, 1988.

———. *Households and Holiness: The Religious Culture of Israelite Women.* Facets. Minneapolis: Fortress, 2005.

Miller, J. Maxwell, and John H. Hayes. *A History of Ancient Israel and Judah.* 2nd ed. Louisville: Westminster John Knox, 2006.

Miller, Patrick D. Jr. "God the Warrior." *Interpretation* 19 (1965) 39–46.

———, and J. J. M. Roberts. *The Hand of the Lord: A Reassessment of the "Ark Narrative" of 1 Samuel.* Johns Hopkins Near Eastern Studies. Baltimore: Johns Hopkins University Press, 1977.

Moran, William. *The Amarna Letters.* Baltimore: Johns Hopkins University Press, 1992.

Muilenburg, James. "The Linguistic and Rhetorical Usages of the Particle *kî* in the Old Testament." In *Hearing and Speaking the Word*, edited by Thomas F. Best, 208–33. Chico, CA: Scholars, 1984.

Myers, Milton L. *The Soul of Modern Economic Man: Ideas of Self-interest, Thomas Hobbes to Adam Smith.* Chicago: University of Chicago Press, 1983.

Nelson, Richard D. *Joshua: A Commentary.* Old Testament Library. Louisville: Westminster John Knox, 1997.

Niditch, Susan. *War in the Hebrew Bible.* Oxford: Oxford University Press, 1993.

Noth, Martin. *The Deuteronomistic History.* Journal for the Study of the Old Testament Supplement Series 15. Sheffield: University of Sheffield, 1981.

Niebuhr, H. Richard. *The Meaning of Revelation.* New York: Macmillan, 1962.

O'Day, Gail R. *Revelation in the Fourth Gospel: Narrative Mode and Theological Claim.* Philadelphia: Fortress, 1986.

Overholt, Thomas W. *Channels of Prophecy: The Social Dynamics of Prophetic Activity.* Minneapolis: Fortress, 1989.

———. *Cultural Anthropology and the Old Testament.* Guides to Biblical Scholarship. Minneapolis: Fortress, 1996.

Polzin, Robert. *Moses and the Deuteronomist: Deuteronomy, Joshua, Judges.* 1980. Reprinted, Indiana Studies in Biblical Literature. Bloomington: Indiana University Press, 1993.

Rad, Gerhard von. *Der heilige Krieg im alten Israel*. Göttingen: Vandenhoeck & Ruprecht, 1958.

———. *Holy War in Ancient Israel*. Translated and edited by Marva J. Dawn. Introduction by Ben C. Ollenburger. 1991. Reprinted, Eugene, OR: Wipf & Stock, 2001.

———. *Old Testament Theology*. Vol. 1: *Theology of Israel's Historical Traditions*. Translated by D. M. G. Stalker. New York: Harper & Row, 1962.

———. *Old Testament Theology*. Vol. 2: *Theology of Israel's Prophetic Traditions*. Translated by D. M. G. Stalker. New York: Harper & Row, 1965.

———. *Wisdom in Israel*. Translated by James D. Martin. Nashville: Abingdon, 1972.

Ricoeur, Paul. *The Conflict of Interpretations*. Evanston: Northwestern University Press, 1974.

———. *Interpretation Theory*. Fort Worth: Texas Christian University Press, 1976.

———. *The Philosophy of Paul Ricoeur*. Edited by Charles E. Reagan and David Stewart. Boston: Beacon, 1978.

Rofé, Alexander. "The Laws of Warfare in the Book of Deuteronomy." *Journal for the Study of the Old Testament* 32 (1985) 28–39.

Rowlett, Lori L. *Joshua and the Rhetoric of Violence: A "New Historicist" Analysis*. Journal for the Study of the Old Testament Supplement Series 226. Sheffield: Sheffield Academic, 1996.

Schafer, Roy. *Language and Insight*. The Sigmund Freud Memorial Lectures 1975–1976. New Haven: Yale University Press, 1978.

Schottroff, Willy, and Wolfgang Stegemann, editors. *God of the Lowly: Socio-historical Interpretations of the Bible*. Translated by Matthew J. O'Connell. Maryknoll, NY: Orbis, 1984.

Schreiter, Robert S. *Constructing Local Theologies*. Maryknoll, NY: Orbis, 1985.

Schüssler Fiorenza, Elisabeth. *Bread Not Stone: The Challenge of Feminist Biblical Interpretation*. Boston: Beacon, 1984.

———. *Rhetoric and Ethic: The Politics of Biblical Studies*. Minneapolis: Fortress, 1999

Schwartz, Regina M. *The Curse of Cain: The Violent Legacy of Monotheism*. Chicago: University of Chicago Press, 1997.

Sobrino, Jon. *The True Church and the Poor*. Translated by Matthew J. O'Connell. 1984. Reprinted, Eugene, OR: Wipf & Stock, 2004.

Spina, Frank A. "The Concept of Social Rage in the Old Testament and the Ancient Near East." PhD dissertation, University of Michigan, 1977.

Stern, P. D. *The Biblical Ḥerem*. Brown Judaic Studies 211. Atlanta: Scholars, 1991.

Sternberg, Meir. *The Poetics of Biblical Narrative: Ideological Literature and the Drama of Reading*. Indiana Literary Biblical Series. Bloomington: Indiana University Press, 1985.

Suggs, M. Jack. *Wisdom, Christology and Law in St. Matthew's Gospel*. Cambridge: Harvard University Press, 1970.

Tracy, David. *The Analogical Imagination: Christian Theology and the Culture of Pluralism*. New York: Crossroad, 1981.

Trible, Phyllis. *God and the Rhetoric of Sexuality*. Overtures to Biblical Theology. Philadelphia: Fortress, 1978.

———. *Rhetorical Criticism: Context, Method, and the Book of Jonah*. Guides to Biblical Scholarship. Minneapolis: Fortress, 1994.

———. *Texts of Terror: Literary-Feminist Readings of Biblical Narratives*. Overtures to Biblical Theology. Philadelphia: Fortress, 1984.

Waldow, H. Eberhard von. "The Concept of War in the Old Testament." *Horizons in Biblical Theology* 6 (1984) 27–48.

Wilder, Amos N. "Story and Story-World." *Interpretation* 37 (1983) 353–64.

Wilson, Robert R. "The Hardening of Pharaoh's Heart." *Catholic Biblical Quarterly* 41 (1979) 18–36.

———. *Sociological Approaches to the Old Testament*. Guides to Biblical Scholarship. Philadelphia: Fortress, 1984.

———. *Prophecy and Society in Ancient Israel*. Philadelphia: Fortress, 1979.

Wolff, Hans Walter. *Hosea*. Translated by Gary Stansell. Hermeneia. Philadelphia: Fortress, 1974.

———. "Micah the Moreshite—The Prophet and His Background." In *Israelite Wisdom*, edited by John G. Gammie, 77–84. Missoula, MT: Scholars, 1978.

———. *Micah the Prophet*. Translated by Ralph D. Gehrke. Philadelphia: Fortress, 1981.

Yoder, John Howard. *Karl Barth and the Problem of War*. Nashville: Abingdon, 1970.

———. *Nevertheless: The Varieties and Shortcomings of Religious Pacifism*. Rev. ed. Scottdale, PA: Herald, 1992.

———. *The Politics of Jesus: Vicit Agnus Noster*. 2nd ed. Grand Rapids: Eerdmans, 1994.

Younger, K. Lawson Jr. *Ancient Conquest Accounts: Study in Ancient Near Eastern and Biblical History*. Journal for the Study of the Old Testament: Supplement Series 98. Sheffield: JSOT Press, 1990.

Index of Ancient Documents

Author Index